WORLD BOOK
looks at

THE
AMERICAN WEST

World Book, Inc.
a Scott Fetzer Company

Chicago   London   Sydney   Toronto

WORLD BOOK
looks at
THE AMERICAN WEST

World Book looks at

Books in this series are based on information and illustrations contained in The World Book Encyclopedia.

Created and edited by Brian Williams and Brenda Williams
Designed by Tim Mayer

World Book, Inc.
525 W. Monroe
Chicago, Illinois 60661

For information on other World Book products, call 1-800-255-1750 x2238

ISBN 0-7166-1805-2 (hard cover)
ISBN 0-7166-1809-5 (soft cover)
Library of Congress Catalog Card Number 96-61140

Printed in Mexico

1 2 3 4 5 6 7 8 9 10 99 98 97 96

CONTENTS

Introducing the American West

The exploration and settlement of the West is one of the most exciting chapters in American history. It is a story of courage and endurance in the face of natural obstacles, of triumphs and tragedies in a vast and beautiful wilderness.

A new nation grows

The Revolutionary War in America (1775-1783) led to the birth of the United States. After the war, Britain gave the new nation rights to almost all the territory between the Appalachian Mountains and the Mississippi River. In 1803, the United States bought the Louisiana territory from France. This purchase almost doubled the size of the United States.

The government sent explorers into the new territory and hardy pioneers began settling in the West. Traders and scouts arrived at the Pacific coast in the early 1800's, and by 1820, frontier settlements reached as far west as the Mississippi River. By the 1830's, settlers had pushed across the Mississippi into what later became the states of Iowa, Missouri, Arkansas, and eastern Texas.

Artists were inspired by the West. *The Bolter*, 1904, an oil painting by Charles Marion Russell, is typical of this artist's scenes of cowboy life.

Puzzled by a new word?

To learn the meaning of a difficult or new word, turn to the glossary on page 62.

The spectacular and rugged landscape of the West includes Monument Valley in southeastern Utah – a favorite location for Western movies.

THE GROWTH OF THE UNITED STATES

1565 Spaniards founded St. Augustine, Florida, the first permanent European settlement in what is now the United States.

1607 English colonists founded Jamestown, the first permanent British settlement in Virginia.

1620 Pilgrims founded Plymouth Colony, the second permanent British settlement in North America.

1776 The American colonists adopted the Declaration of Independence and formed the United States of America.

1803 The Louisiana Purchase of territory from France almost doubled the size of the United States at a cost of about $15 million.

1845 Texas joined the United States.

1846 Britain gave the southern part of the Oregon Country to the United States.

1848 Victory in the Mexican War (1846-1848) gave the United States vast new territory in the West.

1849 The California Gold Rush started.

1861-1865 Civil War raged between the Northern and Southern states.

1862 The Homestead Act encouraged settlers to move west.

1869 The Union Pacific and Central Pacific railroads met in Utah, creating the first transcontinental railroad.

1890 The Indian wars were practically over. The U.S. Census officially recognized the fact that America's frontier days had ended.

A pioneer family home was often a log cabin. Where wood was plentiful, settlers cut trees into logs to build the sides of the house. The cabin shown here does not yet have a complete roof.

Across the Plains

The land beyond, called the Great Plains, was dry and treeless, and seemed to be poor farmland. Native Americans, or Indians, lived on the plains by hunting buffalo. However, explorers, traders, and fur trappers told of rich farmland and forests beyond the Rocky Mountains. For land-hungry people, the West seemed a promised land.

By the 1840's, thousands of settlers were moving westward across the Great Plains. Many of these pioneers settled beyond the country's western boundary. Some went to find land and to build homes for their families. Others went in search of riches, dreaming of gold and silver. One of the world's great migrations had begun – and with it, the legend of the West.

The Louisiana Purchase of 1803 added the territory between the Mississippi River and the Rocky Mountains to the United States.

More and more Americans

- In 1783, at the end of the Revolutionary War, there were just over 3 million people in the United States.

- By 1819, there were 9.3 million Americans.

- By 1849, this figure had risen to 22 million.

- By 1869, there were almost 39 million Americans, of whom nearly 7 million lived west of the Mississippi River.

- By 1890, nearly 17 million people lived west of the Mississippi. The population of the United States neared 100 million in 1916.

The pioneers

The pioneers who opened the West played an important part in the development of the United States. They provided information about the area's geography, travel routes, and future commercial possibilities. They changed the look of the land as they cleared the wilderness to build farms, roads, and towns. The settlement of the West also led to the loss of Native American lands and brought an end to the traditional ways of life of many American Indians.

Tepees were the homes of Plains Indians. This 1800's drawing by Karl Bodmer, a Swiss artist, shows an Assiniboine camp. A tepee was made by stretching buffalo skins over a framework of wooden poles. Plains Indians hunted buffalo on horseback. The woman in the foreground is loading a travois, a wooden frame with shafts pulled by a dog.

A Blackfoot chief of the Plains.
This oil painting by George Catlin shows a chief named *Stu-mick-o-sucks* ("The Buffalo Bull's Back Fat").

The fate of the Indians

As the settlers moved westward, they took over much of the land that Native Americans had occupied for thousands of years. Fighting often broke out between the pioneers and the Indians. The United States government sent soldiers to battle the Indians and the soldiers won most of these so-called Indian Wars. By the mid-1800's, the government had moved almost all the Eastern Indians west of the Mississippi. Indians in the West then faced growing pressure from settlers moving onto their lands.

The westward movement

The long process of settling the United States from coast to coast drew to a close after the Civil War (1861-1865). In 1862, Congress passed the Homestead Act, which offered Western land to settlers at little or no cost. Thousands of hopeful Americans went west to start farms. Many recent immigrants from Europe and elsewhere settled on the Great Plains, which – contrary to earlier reports – included much excellent farmland. Miners flocked to the West as the demand for minerals soared. Towns sprang up near the mines. After the Civil War, cattle-ranching spread throughout the Southwest.

Herds of buffalo roamed the Great Plains. Today, only remnants of those vast herds remain. These buffalo graze in Custer State Park, South Dakota.

Introduction

Americans moved westward by the thousands during the early 1800's. An 1837 painting shows a wagon train encountering a mirage. For many settlers, struggling to cross rivers, plains, and mountains, their longed-for new home seemed just a dream.

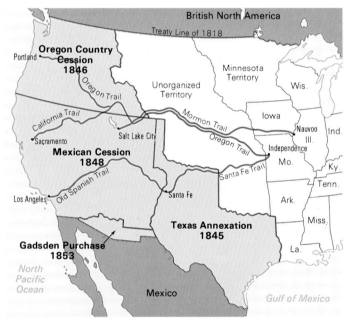

This map shows how America grew. By the mid-1800's, its western frontier reached the Pacific Ocean. The Oregon Country was handed over to the United States by Britain. The rest of the new territory came from Mexico.

The end of a way of life

The settlement of the West brought an end to the Native American way of life. Farmers fenced in much of the land. Settlers moving west slaughtered the buffalo herds on which Plains Indians depended for survival. When Indians fought against the settlers, the government again sent soldiers to crush the uprisings. The government pushed more and more Indians onto reservations. By 1900, the Native American way of life had become a thing of the past.

Dreams and dramas

This book tells how the West was explored and settled. The story of the American West is a story of dreams and dramas, of hardships and dangers. It tells of lonely pioneers struggling to build new lives far from the civilization they had known in the East. It is the story of the clash of peoples, as the settlers moved onto lands where Native Americans lived.

The settlement of the West resulted from the dreams of gold-hungry prospectors, and of homesteaders who toiled to transform the barren plains into fields of grain. It is the story of cowboys riding the open range, of Native Americans defending their tribal homelands, and of settlers building towns in the wilderness. It is the story of lawmen and outlaws, and of epic journeys across mountains, prairies, and deserts on horseback and in covered wagons.

The legend lives

The West was more than just a brief episode in history. It became one of the most powerful expressions of American culture. Through art, movies, and stories, the West became part of the culture of the world.

Plains Indians were at home in the wilderness. These Assiniboine hunters moved swiftly on snowshoes. Here, they have closed in on a buffalo bogged down in the deep snow.

Painter of the Indians

George Catlin (1796-1872) was known for his paintings and drawings of Native Americans. From 1830 to 1836, he spent several summers among various Indian tribes in the West, making almost 500 portraits and sketches. Later, from 1852 to 1857, he painted Indians living west of the Rocky Mountains. Several of George Catlin's pictures appear in this book.

The Trailblazers

In the 1700's, as the new nation of the United States was born, hardy frontiersmen blazed new trails into unexplored territory. These bold adventurers included Daniel Boone.

Frontier explorers built log rafts. Travel by water was easier than by land.

Daniel Boone (1734-1820) was one of the most famous pioneers in U.S. history. He journeyed through the rugged wilderness of the Appalachian Mountains in 1769 and reached the unexplored area that became known as Kentucky. He cleared the Wilderness Road, a trail that created a route to the West for thousands of settlers.

Boone was raised on a farm in Pennsylvania. He learned to hunt and shoot a rifle as a child. He was always restless. After his marriage, he was forever yearning to move on, to find new lands deeper in the woods. He reached Kentucky by following an Indian trail and found vast buffalo herds, deer and turkey in the woods, and meadows ideal for farming. He built a fort and a cabin for his family, founding a village named Boonesborough.

Battling with Indians

Boone and his family had many encounters with Indians. In 1773, his oldest son was captured and killed by Indians. In 1776, he led an expedition to rescue his daughter and two other young women who had been taken captive by Indian warriors.

Trappers in the wilderness hunted beaver, as shown in this 1858 painting. They sold the pelts (animal skins) or traded them for food and other supplies.

Johnny Appleseed

Johnny Appleseed was the name given to John Chapman (1774-1845), an American pioneer who planted apple trees along the early frontier.

- **From 1797 until his death, he wandered alone through Ohio and Indiana.**

- **According to the story, he gave apple seeds and apple saplings to everyone he met.**

- **Johnny Appleseed became a folk hero as the result of stories and poems about him, though most of these deeds were probably imaginary.**

Daniel Boone leads settlers through the Cumberland Gap, a mountain pass on the Wilderness Road from Virginia to Kentucky. This 1852 painting is the work of George Caleb Bingham.

TRUE STORY? TALL STORY?

Daniel Boone wore a coonskin cap.

Not true. He usually wore a black felt hat. His hair was long, and tied in a ponytail.

The Indians called Boone "Big Turtle."

True. Chief Blackfish of the Shawnee adopted Boone as his son and named him *Shel-tow-ee* ("Big Turtle").

Boone used tobacco leaves as a weapon.

True. In 1782, Indians surprised Boone in a tobacco loft. He jumped down among them, throwing an armful of tobacco leaves. The dust in the leaves choked and blinded the Indians and Boone fled into the woods.

In 1778, Boone himself was captured by Shawnee Indians. They forced him to "run the gauntlet." He had to run between two lines of warriors, who tried to beat him with clubs and other weapons as he ran. Boone ran in a zigzag pattern, head-down, and butted the last warrior in the chest, running over him to safety. Boone was accepted as a Shawnee brave and stayed with the Indians, but escaped when he learned the Shawnee planned to attack Boonesborough. He journeyed for four days to warn the settlers, who took refuge inside the fort. For nine days, the Indians attacked the fort, before finally giving up.

Far from the crowd

Four years later, Boone lost another of his sons in an Indian ambush. In 1799, he left Kentucky for Missouri, which was then Spanish territory. Asked why he was going, Boone answered, "Too many people! Too crowded! Too crowded! I want more elbow room." He never stayed long in one place, and continued to hunt and explore the West, even as an old man with failing eyesight.

French fur traders were among the first whites to explore the West. In 1742, the brothers Vérendrye may have been the first Europeans to reach the Rocky Mountains. They explored the Missouri River in what is now South Dakota. In 1743, they buried a small lead plate near present-day Fort Pierre as proof of their visit. The plate was found in 1913.

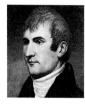

William Clark (1770-1838) was a mapmaker. Like Lewis, he had experience of the wilderness and of fighting Indians. Charles Wilson Peale painted Clark (left) in 1810.

Meriwether Lewis (1774-1809), a U.S. army captain and private secretary to President Thomas Jefferson, was the expedition naturalist. This portrait of Lewis (right) was painted in 1807 by Charles Wilson Peale.

The Explorers

Explorers and scouts made their way across the West in the early 1800's. These brave pathfinders helped map the routes for settlers to follow.

Across the Rocky Mountains

The first government-backed exploration of the West began in May 1804, when the Lewis and Clark expedition left a camp near St. Louis, Missouri. About 50 men traveled up the Missouri River in a large, flat-bottomed keelboat and two dugout canoes. The explorers spent the winter in what is now North Dakota, near the villages of the Mandan and Hidatsa Indians.

In the spring of 1805, the party split: 33 people continued west while the rest returned to St. Louis with reports and maps of their discoveries. Crossing the mountains, the explorers went hungry until they killed and ate some of their pack horses. They built canoes to travel down the Clearwater, Snake, and Columbia rivers to the Pacific coast, which they reached in November 1805. There they built a fort and spent the winter.

In March 1806, Lewis and Clark led separate parties on different routes for the return east. The explorers met up again on the Missouri in August and returned to St. Louis in September 1806.

The Lewis and Clark expedition. The map shows where the explorers spent the winters of 1804-1805 and 1805-1806, and the different routes taken by Lewis and Clark for part of their return journey.

The Clark Connection

William Clark was the younger brother of George Rogers Clark, a soldier who became a national hero fighting the British during the Revolutionary War. In 1783, Thomas Jefferson asked the older Clark to explore the West, but Clark refused. Soon after Jefferson became President in 1801, he planned a new expedition and chose Meriwether Lewis to lead the explorers. Lewis selected William Clark, an old army friend, to share the leadership with him.

The Rocky Mountains were a natural barrier to explorers seeking routes west to the Pacific Ocean.

A FAMOUS FRONTIERSMAN

Jim Bridger (1804-1881) was born in Virginia. He spent 40 years in the West working as a hunter, trapper, fur trader, and guide.

- **In 1824, while searching for furs in the Rocky Mountains, he was probably the first white person to see the Great Salt Lake.**

- **He was also one of the first white people to see the wonders of the land that became Yellowstone National Park.**

- **In 1843, he built Fort Bridger in Wyoming as a way station to supply pioneers on the Oregon Trail.**

- **He helped plan overland stage routes and scouted for the army. In the 1860's, Bridger was the first person to measure the Bozeman Trail, about 600 miles (970 kilometers) from Fort Laramie, Wyoming, to Virginia City, Montana. The trail was used by gold seekers.**

- **Jim Bridger died near Kansas City in 1881.**

Sacagawea (1787?-1812), a Shoshone Indian woman, acted as interpreter to the Lewis and Clark expedition. In 1805, the explorers met a band of Shoshones whose chief was Sacagawea's brother. A Shoshone guide helped the explorers cross the Bitterroot Mountains along what is now the Idaho-Montana border.

Way to the West

From a journey of about 8,000 miles (12,800 kilometers), Lewis and Clark returned with maps of the frontier and information about the region's natural resources and the Indian tribes who lived there. The knowledge gained by the expedition enabled the United States to claim the Oregon Country, and made possible the great pioneer movement that settled the West during the 1800's.

Kit Carson (1809-1868)

Carson and Frémont

In the 1840's, John Charles Frémont explored the area between the Rocky Mountains and the Pacific Ocean. Frémont was an army surveyor, and his guide was the frontier scout Christopher (Kit) Carson. They visited Oregon and California, which was then a Mexican province. Frémont helped produce the first scientific map of the American West.

John Charles Frémont (1813-1890)

The Indians

Inside a Mandan chief's home, or lodge. The chief smokes his pipe in the company of his horses and dogs. Utensils and weapons hang from the wooden beams and posts that support the domed roof. This painting was made in the early 1800's by Swiss artist Karl Bodmer.

The story of the Native Americans began thousands of years ago. Their ancestors came to the New World from Asia. Most experts believe they arrived at least 15,000 years ago.

Indians or Native Americans?

When Christopher Columbus arrived in the New World in 1492, there were probably about 15 million to 20 million people living in North America north of Mexico. Columbus called these people Indians because he thought he had reached the Indies (in Asia). However, almost every Indian group had its own name, and many Indians refer to themselves today as Native Americans.

First contacts

Early contacts between Indians of the East and European explorers were often friendly. The Europeans followed Indian trails, and the Indians taught them to make snowshoes, toboggans, and to travel by canoe. They showed them how to grow corn, potatoes, and squash, and introduced the whites to tobacco.

The Europeans brought metal tools, guns, and liquor, as well as cattle and horses, which were unknown to the Indians.

As Europeans took more land for their own, often unfairly, warfare between the two groups became common. In addition, many Indians died from measles, smallpox, and other diseases brought by Europeans.

The Plains Indians

As the settlers moved westward beyond the Mississippi, they met the Plains Indians. Few Indians lived in this vast grassland before the arrival of the Europeans. Most of the original Plains Indians lived in villages along the rivers. Women tended crops of beans, corn, squash, and tobacco, while men hunted deer, and sometimes buffalo.

INDIAN HOMES

Apache brush lodge

Paiute wickiup

Omaha earth lodge

Wichita grass house

Navajo hogan

Sioux buffalo-hide tepee

Indians in North America built many kinds of homes.

Some Indians covered a pole framework with leaves or tree bark, like the dome-shaped wigwam of the Northeast.

The Apache and Paiute of the Southwest used brush and matting to make simple wickiups.

The Pawnee and some other tribes lived in earth lodges, built in pits and roofed with sod.

Poles or logs covered with soil formed the Navajo hogan.

Plains Indians built cone-shaped tepees of buffalo skins.

Buffalo hunters

Buffalo were difficult to hunt on foot, but after the Spaniards brought horses to the Plains in the 1600's, the Indians could follow the great herds of buffalo on horseback. Buffalo meat became their main food. On the eastern Plains, Indians continued to live in earth lodges and farm part of the year. But on the western Plains, the buffalo hunters were always on the move. They lived in large tepees, which could be moved easily from camp to camp.

A Comanche village. A painting by George Catlin shows women curing buffalo hides. Meat is drying on poles in the sun. The Indians found many uses for buffalo skins. They stretched the skins over poles to form tepees. It took between 15 and 30 buffalo hides to make one tepee.

Indians enjoyed playing games. This painting of *Winter Games of the Cheyenne* by Dick West shows stone-tossing and "stick in the hoop" among other games. Women are playing shinny, a kind of field hockey, while people in the background toboggan on sleds.

The Far West

In the Far West, other groups of Indians lived mainly by hunting, fishing, and plant-gathering. Some tribes, such as the Shoshone of the Great Basin, moved onto the Plains when they obtained horses, and began to hunt buffalo.

Farmers and fighters

The Pueblo lived in the Southwest. These people grew corn, beans, and squash, and raised turkeys. They built many-storied houses of adobe (sun-dried mud) and rock. Pueblo houses were home to many families, and protected them against raids by the Apache and Navajo. These tribes were fierce fighters, who depended chiefly on hunting and gathering for their food.

Indian Life

Native American beliefs and ways of life had developed over many centuries. In the early 1800's, some Indians in the West had never seen a white person.

Living together

Many Indians lived in bands of between 20 and 500 people. Others lived in larger groups known as tribes. Members of a tribe spoke the same language and had the same religious beliefs. Tribes might have one or more leaders, known as chiefs. In some tribes, one chief might be leader during peacetime. Another would lead the tribe in war. Decisions were usually made by general agreement after a meeting of a council made up of the wisest and most respected members of the tribe.

Family life

Many Indians married young – girls between 13 and 15, boys between 15 and 20. Boys and girls did not go to school. Instead, they learned the skills they would need by helping their parents and older brothers and sisters. They learned the history of their people by listening to stories, which they in turn passed on to their children.

Rock carvings were made by Indians living in Arizona several thousand years ago. The carvings on Newspaper Rock in Petrified Forest National Park have never been translated.

The sun dance was a religious ritual of the Sioux, in which young men demonstrated their courage by attaching strings to their chests and tugging until they tore free. Sun dance ceremonies often lasted several days.

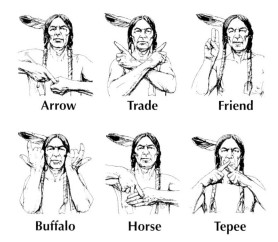

Arrow **Trade** **Friend**

Buffalo **Horse** **Tepee**

Indian sign language
Many languages were spoken on the Plains. Since there was no common language, Plains Indians often communicated by signs. The arrows show the direction of hand movements.

SWEATING IT OUT

Many Indian tribes had a sweat lodge ceremony. The sweat lodge was a heated building. Some sweat lodges were heated by a fire. In others, water was poured over heated stones to produce steam. People went into the sweat lodge to perspire in the heat. They believed this influenced spirits and cleansed the body of illness.

Navajo Indians weaving. This painting, by a modern Navajo artist, shows the dress still worn by Navajo women. The Navajo learned weaving from the Pueblo Indians. Blankets are made by Navajo people in Arizona, New Mexico, and Utah.

Craft skills

Indians were skilled at crafts such as basketry, carving, and pottery. Many Indians made their own clothes from animal skins and fur. Tanned deer hide, known as buckskin, was a popular material for making clothes. The Pueblo of the Southwest were expert weavers of cotton cloth. The Navajo took up wool weaving later and became famous for their blankets and rugs.

The spirit world

Indians had no single religion, but certain beliefs were widespread. Most important was the belief in a mysterious force in nature. This "spirit power" could be gained by certain people or through certain ceremonies. Some tribes believed in a "great spirit," an especially powerful god. The spirit world could be reached with the aid of a shaman, a person believed to have close contact with the unseen world. Shamans were sometimes called medicine men or medicine women because they also treated the sick.

INDIAN MEDICINE

Some Indians believed that diseases were caused by an object in the body. Shamans began their cure for such conditions with special songs and movements.

- They blew tobacco smoke over the sick person because tobacco was believed to have magical powers.

- Shamans sucked on the body of the sick person until they "found" the object believed to be causing the illness. Then they spat out the object – usually a small stick or stone hidden in the shaman's mouth.

- Shamans set broken bones and used herb remedies. Many plants used by Indians are in medical products today.

Rings of stones were laid out by Indians to track the movement of the sun and stars. This ring in Wyoming is called the Bighorn Medicine Wheel, and dates from about A.D. 1400.

Hunters of the Plains

A buffalo and calf. The buffalo is a herd animal. Millions of buffalo roamed the Plains in these herds.

The Plains Indians hunted buffalo for food, but the buffalo provided much more than meat. It was the mainstay of life for the Indians.

The buffalo

The American bison, or "buffalo," is a large wild ox. A full-grown bull (male) may measure over 10 feet (3 meters) from nose to tail, and a very big bull can weigh up to 3,000 pounds (1,400 kilograms).

Great herds of buffalo roamed North America between the Appalachian Mountains on the east and the Rocky Mountains on the west. In 1850, about 20 million bison roamed across the Plains. Huge herds often held up railroad trains.

Following the buffalo

For the Plains Indians, daily life was ruled by the movements of the buffalo herds. Buffalo hunters were always on the move, following the animals. When they changed camp, Plains Indians used dogs to pull loads on a wooden frame called a travois. Later, they used horses to pull the travois. The hunters were expert riders, shooting

THE SIOUX

The Sioux, who lived throughout the northern Plains, were famous for their bravery, fighting ability, and political skills.

- The Sioux had many divisions.

- The Santee, or Dakota, Sioux lived in what is now Minnesota.

- The Yankton, or Nakota, Sioux lived in the eastern Dakotas. Both groups hunted and farmed.

- The Lakota, or Teton, Sioux hunted buffalo in the western Dakotas and in Nebraska.

Buffalo hunters rode at full speed, as shown in this George Catlin painting (about 1835) of *Indians Hunting Buffalo with Bows and Lances.*

Mandan Indians danced to ensure success in hunting buffalo. The Mandan Indians lived in the North Dakota region. Swiss artist Karl Bodmer recorded this buffalo dance in the 1830's.

How did Indians preserve meat?

The Indians ate fresh buffalo meat roasted over a fire.

To preserve meat, they dried it in the sun to make jerky.

They also mixed dried meat with hot fat and berries to make a food called pemmican.

buffalo with bow and arrow or gun while riding bareback at a gallop.

The Plains Indians depended on the buffalo for food and shelter. They used buffalo skins to make winter clothing and bedding, as well as their tepees. They used the bones and horns to make tools and utensils, and they dried the buffalo dung for fuel. A good buffalo hunter might have two or more wives to prepare all the buffalo hides he brought home. The Plains Indians held many ceremonies aimed at ensuring a large enough supply of buffalo.

The Plains Indians

Major tribes of the Plains region included:

Arapaho	Iowa
Arikara	Kansa
Assiniboine	Kiowa
Blackfoot	Mandan
Cheyenne	Omaha
Comanche	Osage
Crow	Pawnee
Gros Ventre	Sioux
Hidatsa	Wichita

Indians hunting buffalo. Before they had horses, the Plains Indians stalked buffalo on foot, or stampeded a herd so that the buffalo tumbled over a cliff. On horseback, the Indians could chase the buffalo. Hunters rode close enough to shoot animals with bows and arrows, as shown in this drawing by Karl Bodmer.

Proud Warriors

War was sometimes the only way in which Indian tribes could settle disputes. Warfare also gave Indians a chance to achieve high rank in their tribes.

The bow and arrow was probably the most common Indian weapon. In battle, Indian warriors also used spears, knives, clubs, and tomahawks.

Counting coup

On the Plains, it was considered braver to touch a living enemy and get away than to kill him. This act was known as counting coup. Warriors on the Plains carried a stick known as a coup stick into battle, and attempted to touch an enemy with it. Warriors who counted coup wore eagle feathers as symbols of their courage.

A Mandan chief in ceremonial dress is shown in a painting by George Catlin. Buffalo horns top his feathered bonnet. Hair from enemy scalps hangs from his clothing. The hand on his shirt shows that he killed an enemy with his bare hands. This chief's name was *Mah-to-toh-pa* ("The Four Bears").

Victory dances celebrated success in battle. Hidatsa Indians of the Northwest tied the scalps of enemies to a pole and danced to drums.

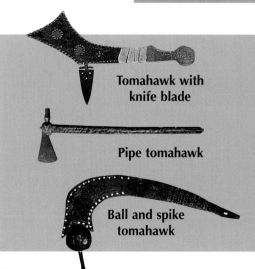

Tomahawk with knife blade

Pipe tomahawk

Ball and spike tomahawk

TOMAHAWKS

Tomahawks were war clubs developed by the Indians of the East. There were many types.

- Some tomahawks ended in a ball or knob.
- Some ended in a flat blade.
- Pipe tomahawks had a pipe bowl on the head and a hollow handle, so they could be smoked.

Scalps of enemy warriors hang from poles in this scene from George Catlin's painting *A Bird's Eye View of the Mandan Village*. A fence protected the village from attack by enemies.

A Sioux chief, painted by George Catlin. Some tribes were led by one chief in time of war and by another chief during peacetime.

A shield used by a Crow chief named Big Bear. Indian shields were made of buffalo hide. The buckskin shield cover was often decorated with symbolic designs.

Taking scalps

The scalp of an enemy was a war trophy in parts of North America. Scalp hunting was encouraged by some Europeans. They paid friendly Indians for the scalps of their enemies.

Initiation

Training for hunting and war began in childhood. After most Indian boys reached their early teens, they went through a test of strength or bravery – an initiation ceremony. Many went without food for a long period or lived alone in the wilderness. In some tribes, a boy was expected to have a vision of the spirit that would become his lifelong guardian.

Was wounded

Killed an enemy   **Rode into the enemy without a weapon**

Feathers were worn to show acts of bravery. Markings on the feather identified the brave deed.

21

The Westward Movement

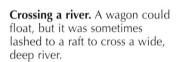

As explorers opened up new routes, traders, trappers, gold prospectors, and settlers began moving westward. They were drawn by reports of riches, and not disheartened by those explorers who found only desert.

The westward movement was more rapid than the United States government expected. In 1801, President Jefferson foresaw a distant time when the continent would be settled from coast to coast. However, pioneers reached California and other regions of the Far West during the 1840's.

Crossing a river. A wagon could float, but it was sometimes lashed to a raft to cross a wide, deep river.

Along the Mississippi

The entire Mississippi Valley became part of the United States with the Louisiana Purchase of 1803. Settlers and traders set out on the river in flatboats, keelboats, and rafts. The coming of steamboats in the early 1800's increased the importance of the Mississippi and Missouri rivers as routes for settlement and trade. Mississippi River cities such as St. Louis, Memphis, and New Orleans served as supply bases for the pioneers setting out on their journey westward.

Some early explorers did not consider the Great Plains fit for settlement. In 1820, Major Stephen H. Long led a small expedition up the Platte River to the Rocky Mountains. He reported that the Great Plains had neither trees nor water. They were so barren that he called the Plains the "Great American Desert."

STEAMING UP THE MISSOURI

Steamboat traffic began on the lower Missouri in 1819. The steamer *Yellowstone* sailed up the Missouri River to Fort Tecumseh (now Fort Pierre, South Dakota) in 1831. The journey proved that steamboats could travel on the upper Missouri. Many pioneers went at least part of the way west on a steamboat.

Mountain men

In 1821, a trader named William Becknell blazed the Santa Fe Trail all the way from Independence, Missouri, to Santa Fe in what is now New Mexico. "Mountain men" such as Jim Bridger, Kit Carson, and Jedediah Smith mapped many areas of the Rockies as they searched for beaver. In 1826, Smith made the first overland trip to California.

A large flatboat could carry two or three families, along with their livestock and everything else they owned.

California settlers

California and Texas were once Mexican provinces. In 1841, the first organized group of American settlers came to California by land. They were led by John Bidwell, a schoolteacher, and John Bartleson, a wagon master and land speculator. More pioneers followed, driving their wagons through the mountain passes. The newcomers wanted California to become part of the United States. Mexico refused to sell California, but gave up the territory after being defeated by American forces in the Mexican War (1846-1848).

Covered wagons carried thousands of pioneers westward. The sturdy Conestoga wagon shown in this 1821 painting by Thomas Birch was drawn by a team of four or six horses.

Austin in Texas

In the early 1820's, the Mexican government had given Stephen F. Austin, a pioneer from Missouri, permission to establish a colony in Texas. By 1835, Americans outnumbered Mexicans in Texas. The Texans rebelled against Mexican rule and gained their independence after the Battle of San Jacinto in 1836. Texas remained an independent republic until 1845, when it joined the United States.

PRAIRIE SCHOONERS

The Conestoga wagon was named for the Conestoga Valley in Pennsylvania, where it was first built by German immigrants in the early 1700's. Later, pioneers crossed the Plains in covered wagons that were much like Conestogas, but smaller and sleeker. From a distance the wagon's white top looked like the sails of a ship, giving it the name "prairie schooner."

Railroads and steamboats were new forms of transportation. This 1834 painting shows travelers in New Jersey transferring from a steamboat to a train.

Pioneer Trails

Routes to the West

To reach the fertile valleys of Oregon or California, the settlers had to cross the Great Plains. The Rocky Mountains rose beyond the Plains, and behind the mountains lay a desertlike region known as the Great Basin.

The weather was also a problem. Heavy rain could wash out a river crossing. Winter snows often made the trail impassable. Summer drought could lead to a shortage of drinking water, less grass for cattle to eat along the way, and more dust to choke the pioneers.

To Oregon and California

Settlers followed the Oregon Trail, which began at Independence, Missouri, and wound westward for about 2,000 miles (3,200 kilometers) across the Great Plains and the Rocky Mountains. The first large group of settlers, about one thousand people, made the Great Migration to Oregon in 1843.

Settlers bound for California split off from the Oregon Trail near Fort Hall, in what is now Idaho. They followed one of several trails southwest to Sacramento. Some settlers took the Santa Fe Trail from Independence to present-day New Mexico. From there, pioneers followed the Old Spanish Trail to Los Angeles.

A wagon train crosses the Medicine Bow River in southeastern Wyoming in an 1870 painting by Samuel Colman.

Pioneers on the trail westward had to cross the deserts and mountains now known as the Badlands of South Dakota.

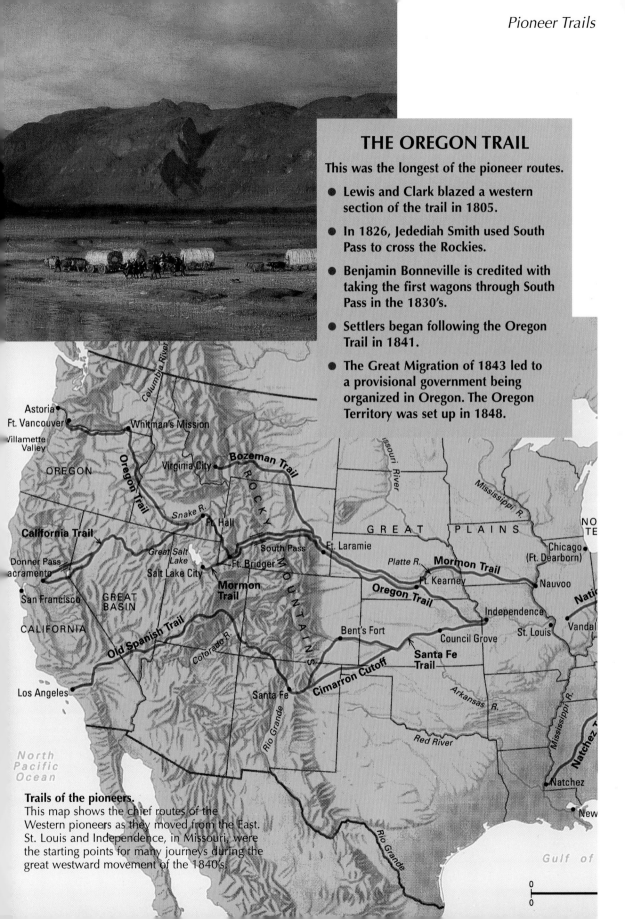

THE OREGON TRAIL

This was the longest of the pioneer routes.

- Lewis and Clark blazed a western section of the trail in 1805.

- In 1826, Jedediah Smith used South Pass to cross the Rockies.

- Benjamin Bonneville is credited with taking the first wagons through South Pass in the 1830's.

- Settlers began following the Oregon Trail in 1841.

- The Great Migration of 1843 led to a provisional government being organized in Oregon. The Oregon Territory was set up in 1848.

Trails of the pioneers.
This map shows the chief routes of the Western pioneers as they moved from the East. St. Louis and Independence, in Missouri, were the starting points for many journeys during the great westward movement of the 1840's.

On the Trail

The journey to the West took four to six months. A family heading for Oregon or California lived in their wagon for most of the trip.

The wagon train

Almost all journeys to the West began in the spring. This gave the pioneers time to get through the western mountains before snow blocked the passes.

The settlers' wagons were pulled by teams of oxen or mules. Settlers brought their prized possessions, farm tools, and enough supplies to last the trip. There were few places along the way where people could buy goods. Often they traded food, clothing, and guns among themselves.

Single men rode on horseback with wagon trains. They herded cattle and sheep, or rode alongside the wagon, helping the driver stay on the trail. Some wagon trains included more than 2,000 cattle and up to 10,000 sheep.

Each wagon train elected a leader, called a captain or wagon master. All wagon trains were guided by a scout.

Indians attacked some wagon trains, but most settlers had a peaceful journey. Very few people traveling west were killed by Indians.

A day on the trail

A day on the trail began shortly before dawn. The pioneers hitched their teams to the wagons and started out. About midday, they stopped for a break, giving pioneers and animals a chance to eat and rest. Then the wagons pressed on to the evening campsite chosen by the scout, where they formed a circle for protection against wild animals and possible Indian attacks. Before bed, the pioneers sat around campfires to eat and talk. Sometimes, if there was a fiddle to play, they sang and danced. Usually, everyone was so tired after a day on the trail that they went to sleep early – ready for the next morning.

A DUSTY, CROWDED TRAIL

Between 1835 and 1855, more than 10,000 people died on the Oregon Trail. Only about 400 of these deaths resulted from Indian attacks. Diseases and firearms accidents were the chief causes of death on the trail. Nor was the journey as lonely as it is described in Western legend.

- **The trail was crowded with wagon trains, army units, missionaries, hunting parties, traders, and even sightseeing tours.**

- **Wagons often camped early in the day to find a good campsite and avoid the crowd.**

Tragedy on the Donner Pass

Most pioneers made the journey without disaster. A few did not. Donner Pass cuts through the Sierra Nevada mountains in eastern California. In the severe winter of 1846-1847, a party of 82 settlers led by George and Jacob Donner became snowbound in the pass cutting through the Sierra Nevada. Only 47 people survived. They built crude shelters of logs, rocks, and hides. They ate twigs, mice, their animals, and their shoes. Finally, the settlers ate their own dead. Fifteen people tried to get through the snow-blocked pass. Seven succeeded, and sent rescuers to bring out the survivors.

The Mormons

The Mormons, a religious community fleeing persecution in Illinois, also headed westward. Brigham Young led the group to the valley of the Great Salt Lake in what is now Utah, arriving at the site of Salt Lake City on July 24, 1847.

A backbreaking climb up a steep riverbank was just one of the difficulties faced by the settlers. Sometimes friendly Plains Indians helped the travelers along the trail to the West.

Life on the Frontier

Frontier forts, like Fort Laramie and Fort Bridger in Wyoming, offered protection and supplies for weary pioneers.

A family camps on the trail. Determined pioneers kept moving until they found a suitable spot to settle.

Food and shelter were the two essentials for pioneers building new lives in a new land. The settlers had to build their own homes, make their own clothes, and grow their own food.

People who went West

Frontier people were a varied mixture. They came from the East Coast, the Middle West, and the South. Some were criminals, running from the law. Some wanted adventure and excitement. Land speculators hoped to get rich quick. But most settlers were farmers, unskilled workers, miners, and former soldiers. Many of these pioneers saw the West as a land of opportunity for themselves and their children.

From far and wide

Large numbers of African Americans moved to the frontier to escape the prejudice they had faced in the East and the South. Mexicans had lived in the Southwest and California since the 1700's. Sheep herders came from France and Spain, miners from Britain, and farmers from Scandinavia and other parts of Europe. Chinese people, who came to build railroads, later drifted to mining camps where they ran laundries, restaurants, and small stores.

In a frontier settlement, men, women, and children worked from dawn to dusk, clearing the land, planting crops, and building homes.

A spinning wheel, brought from the East, was a treasure on the frontier. With a spinning wheel, a pioneer could spin the yarn needed to make clothing for the family.

Making candles was a regular chore. The pioneers twisted string or strips of cloth into wicks, dipped them repeatedly into hot animal fat, then hung the candles to cool and harden.

What was a straddlebug?

On the Great Plains, land sales agents or locators picked out the best sites for farms. They marked their claims with three boards fastened together like the poles of an Indian tepee. These markers were called straddlebugs.

The homesteaders

After 1862, thousands of other families were drawn to the West by the Homestead Act. This law provided that anyone over 21 who was the head of a family and a citizen – or a foreigner who intended to become a citizen – could obtain title (legal right) to 160 acres (65 hectares) of public land. All the homesteader had to do was live on the land for five years and improve it, or pay a small price for ownership.

This law was intended to increase the settlement of "worthless" land, and help workers obtain small farms of their own. The Homestead Act provided farms and new homes for 400,000 to 600,000 families.

Rough and tough

Few people who came to the Great Plains were prepared for the wilderness. They had no understanding of the Indians and little protection against Indian attacks. Some pioneers had never used a gun. Others found that when on horseback, they could not use the long rifles they had carried in the woods back East.

Water and trees were scarce on the Plains. Farm crops withered and died when rains failed. In some areas there was not enough wood for homes, fuel, and fences. It was hard to make a living on small farms and some settlers soon gave up. They did not find the better life they expected. Life on the frontier could be tough.

The pioneer cabin was a workshop as well as a home. All the furniture in this typical pioneer home was made by the settlers. In the evening, by firelight, the family is still at work. The mother is grating corn, while the father repairs a farm tool. Pegs in the wall near the door form a ladder to the loft, where the boys sleep.

Settlers helped one another with tasks such as cornhusking. Teams competed to see which group could husk a pile of corn ears first.

Clothing

For the first year or two on the frontier, people wore the clothing they had brought with them. After these clothes wore out, they made their own. Men wore cowhide boots, trousers or overalls, a wool shirt, a jacket or vest, and a felt hat. Not everyone had socks. A man often wore a red cotton handkerchief around his neck for protection against the dust and cold. Women wore sunbonnets and simple cotton dresses. Some men traded with Indians for deerskin clothes. Because deerskin became cold and stiff when wet, frontiersmen usually wore a shirt and underwear of coarse cloth.

FRONTIER FOOD

- Pioneers ground corn into meal and made corn bread. Roasted ears of corn were a special treat.

- They used wheat flour to make sourdough biscuits, bread, and flapjacks or pancakes.

- They ate dried beans, and meat – game such as buffalo, deer, and wild birds, bacon, salt pork, and dried meat, or jerky.

- Frontier settlers rarely ate fresh fruit and vegetables or dairy products. Ranchers ate beef, and sheepherders ate mutton. But cowboys did not milk cows!

Old Len Martin of Carson City, Nevada, declared while stewing a chicken that there was no sense "picking a chicken too darned close – anybody that don't like the feathers can skin 'em off."

Religion

In the early 1800's, missionaries had pushed into the Far West to preach Christianity to the Indians, but many pioneers lived far from the missions. They relied on preachers called circuit riders, who moved about constantly. When a circuit rider arrived at a settlement, he preached sermons and conducted marriages, baptisms, and other services for people who had sometimes waited many weeks.

Health

Disease was a great danger on the frontier. There were few doctors. Pioneer women relied on a combination of home remedies and folk cures to treat illnesses. Smallpox was the most feared disease. Many communities suffered outbreaks of cholera, malaria, and yellow fever, and nearly everyone was affected at one time or another by a malarial fever called ague. Childhood diseases such as whooping cough, diphtheria, and scarlet fever were common. Many women died in childbirth and many children died at birth or in infancy.

Children did many chores. Grinding corn was often the boys' task. One type of mill consisted of two stones. Corn poured between the stones was ground into a coarse meal when the top stone was turned.

FRONTIER FUN

- Pioneers amused themselves with square dances, cornhusking contests, and nut-gathering parties.

- Women enjoyed quilting parties, making quilts for bedcovers.

- Settlers always enjoyed a house-raising. The men gathered to help build a new house. They stopped work now and then to run races, wrestle, or take part in shooting contests.

- A wedding was a special time for fun and celebrations. The pioneers liked to play tricks on a couple about to be married. Sometimes the women "kidnapped" the bride, while the men rode off with the groom. Of course, both were allowed to escape in time for the wedding.

A school was often one of the first buildings in a new settlement. The school had few books. The children sat on long wooden benches or at homemade desks and repeated lessons given by the teacher.

Pioneer people

Most frontier people fell into two classes. "Solid folk" settled down if they liked the life, or went home if they did not. "Boomers" were always heading for a new boom town. They seldom stayed long enough to make much money, and often wasted what money they had.

The frontier was a world where the jack-of-all-trades flourished. Wyatt Earp was a law officer, buffalo hunter, stagecoach driver, and gambler. Hank Monk, a famous stagecoach driver, also mined and rode the Pony Express. George Jackson, said to have discovered the first gold in the Rockies, was a sheepherder, prospector, farm hand, and miner who later became a businessman.

Trees provided wood for building homes. Pioneers split logs with a mallet and several wedges. The thick slabs of wood were used for flooring, or to build tables, benches, and stools.

A settler kept a rifle for hunting and defense. The Sharps buffalo rifle was a long-range hunting weapon.

31

Most gold seekers headed west overland.

Gold Rush

In 1848, gold was discovered in California. Soon thousands of people were heading for the West, hoping to strike it rich. This was the great Gold Rush.

The Forty-Niners

John A. Sutter, a pioneer trader, had owned land in the Sacramento Valley since 1839. He hired James W. Marshall to help build a sawmill on the American River. In 1848, at Sutter's Mill, Marshall found the first gold nuggets. News of the find spread quickly, and gold seekers from all over the world came to California. They were known as "Forty-Niners."

The first Forty-Niners came to San Francisco on the steamship *California* in February 1849. More ships followed. Some gold seekers sailed the Atlantic Ocean to Panama, crossed overland to the Pacific coast, and made another sea voyage to San Francisco. Others made the long voyage around the tip of South America.

However, most gold seekers headed west overland. They rode horses or mules, or jolted in covered wagons along the Oregon Trail, across the Rockies, and then branched off south along the California Trail.

The largest single silver nugget ever found in North America was discovered at Aspen, Colorado, in 1890. It weighed 1,840 pounds (835 kilograms).

Boom time

The number of people in California grew from about 15,000 in early 1848 to nearly 100,000 by the end of 1849. San Francisco, the gateway to the gold fields, grew from a small town to a bustling city almost overnight.

Miners who found gold spent their money freely. But only a few Forty-Niners struck it rich. Most searched for gold for several years, then gave up. Some went back home, disappointed. Others stayed as farmers and ranchers in California which, in September 1850, became the 31st state of the Union.

Gold rush prospectors. Gold seekers from all over the world came to California.

Pike and his Peak

Snow-capped Pikes Peak in Colorado was named for the explorer Zebulon Montgomery Pike (1779-1813). In 1806, Pike was following the Arkansas River when he spotted the mountain. He climbed partway up the peak but lack of supplies forced him to turn back. He then turned south along the Rio Grande into Spanish territory (now New Mexico). Pikes Peak was climbed by a party led by Major Stephen H. Long in 1820.

The Grand Peak, a 1967 painting of Pikes Peak by James Disney. Zebulon Pike spotted the mountain from a distance of at least 150 miles (241 kilometers).

"Pikes Peak or Bust"

Several parts of the West saw mining booms in the years 1850 to 1880. The rush to Colorado began in 1858, when gold was found along Cherry Creek, near present-day Denver. Gold hunters pushing westward looked for Pikes Peak, probably the most famous mountain in the Rockies. "Pikes Peak or Bust" became the slogan of prospectors heading for the gold fields.

Prospectors lived in camps on the gold fields. This 1865 painting by A.D.O. Bowere shows a mining camp.

Other strikes

Gold rushes drew miners to Montana in 1862. Silver was found in Arizona, where there was a giant silver strike in 1877 at Tombstone. More gold was found around Virginia City in western Nevada. The last great gold rush took place in the Black Hills of South Dakota in 1874 and 1875. Deadwood, a town founded in 1876, became famous as one of the last mining camps of the frontier.

Riders of the Range

A cattle drive in Kansas. Texas ranchers sent their herds to the railroads in Kansas. Dodge City, Abilene, and Wichita became busy cow towns.

The cowboy is part of American folklore. Yet the great days of the cowboy lasted only about 20 years, from the 1860's to the 1880's.

Cowboys on horseback tended great herds of cattle roaming vast stretches of unfenced land. This land was the open range. To Easterners, the life of a cowboy seemed glamorous and exciting. But cowboys' lives were often difficult, dangerous, and – at times – even dull.

Lost without a lariat

American cowboys learned their trade from Mexican cowboys, called *vaqueros*. The Mexican rider's rope, *la reata* in Spanish, became the cowboy's lariat. This rope was the cowboy's most important tool. He used it to catch cattle, to pull animals out of the mud, to tie up horses, and to drag wood to a campfire.

Nat Love was one of many black cowboys. He was born a slave in 1854 but left his home in Tennessee when he was 15 years old. He worked as a cowboy in Kansas until 1889. Nat Love was nicknamed "Deadwood Dick" after he won a riding, roping, and shooting contest in Deadwood, South Dakota. In 1890, he became a railroad porter. He died in 1921.

HOLD ON TO YOUR HAT

A cowboy's hat did more than keep his hair dry.

- **The hat had a wide brim to keep rain, snow, and sun off the rider's face.**

- **The air space in the hat's deep crown kept the cowboy's head cool.**

- **A cowboy could use his hat to fan a fire, signal to other cowboys, or scoop up water from a stream.**

Cowboy clothing

A coat could get in the way, so a cowboy wore one only in bitter cold weather. Most cowboys wore a vest over a shirt. A cowboy wore chaps (from the Spanish *chaparajos*) to protect his legs from thorny brush and from rubbing during long hours in the saddle. Chaps were leather trousers, without a seat, and were worn over other trousers. Cowboys wore leather gloves to prevent rope burns.

Cowboy boots had high heels to keep them from slipping through the stirrups. The heel was tapered so that the rider's foot did not catch in the stirrup if he fell from his horse.

A cowboy wore a neckerchief tied around his neck. It could be pulled over his nose to keep out wind and dust.

Were cowboys crack shots?

Not many cowboys could shoot straight. Few cowboys had money to spend on bullets for practice. Most of the time, a cowboy did not carry a gun. On a trail drive, a cowboy kept a gun tucked in his bedroll to shoot rattlesnakes or kill a horse with a broken leg.

A cowboy on horseback. The image of the cowboy has inspired many artists. This 1904 painting, *Through the Alkali*, is by C. M. Russell.

Cowboys at Work

Cowboys worked from sunup to sundown. They got to town about once a month, usually on payday. Roundup and the trail drive were two events that broke the humdrum routine of life on the ranch.

Branding cattle. Cowboys gave each newborn calf the same brand as its mother.

Roundup

The roundup took place each spring and autumn. On the open range, cattle roamed free, and animals from several ranches became mixed together. At roundup, cowboys from each ranch rode out to collect their own stock. They drove the cattle to a central point and sorted them out according to their brand.

Newborn calves were branded with their owner's mark. The red-hot branding iron left a permanent scar on the animal's hide. Cattle were also marked with a knife cut on the ear – earmarks were often easier to spot than brands. Cattle to be sold for beef were cut, or separated, from the herd by riders on well-trained cutting horses.

Me and Emma   Bar N Bar   Rocking Chair   Running W

Brands on cattle showed who owned the animals. Branding also made it more difficult for rustlers (cattle thieves) to steal cattle and sell them as their own.

Texas longhorn cattle were strong and fierce. They were descended from cattle brought to America by the Spanish.

COW PONIES

Most cowboys rode horses that belonged to the ranch owner. A good cow pony had to be swift and strong.

- The horses used on the range were called mustangs or broncos.

- Mustangs were descended from horses that Spanish explorers brought to North America in the 1500's, and which later ran wild.

- Wild mustangs had to be tamed, or broken, before they could be ridden. A bronco buster was a cowboy who could cure a mustang of bucking when a rider sat on its back.

Trail drive

A trail drive could be as long as 1,000 miles (1,600 kilometers), from the range to the nearest railroad station, where the cattle were shipped to markets in the East. Cattle were collected from several ranches and turned over to a trail boss. He hired 10 or 12 cowboys to handle the herd, which might have as many as 3,000 cattle. The trail boss also hired a cook to drive the chuck wagon and a wrangler to look after the 50 or more horses needed on the drive.

Looking after the herd

Longhorn cattle were tough. They ate almost any kind of plant, and heat and hunger did not bother them. They could go three or four days without water. But cowboys had to be alert for danger that might panic the herd. A river crossing could scare animals into swimming in circles. A sudden noise or a thunderstorm might frighten jittery cattle into stampeding. To stop a stampede, the cowboys raced in front of the herd. They waved their hats and fired guns in the air to turn back the leading cattle.

Journey's end

At the end of the trail drive, the cattle were sold and loaded onto a train. Then the cowboys were paid their wages. In town, a cowboy usually wanted a shave, a haircut, a bath, and clean clothes. Next, he wanted a good meal before he headed for the nearest saloon.

The chuck wagon carried food, cooking pots, drinking water, and the men's bedrolls. These wagons were used on a trail drive and for roundups on the range. Meals were often beans, bacon, and biscuits.

Stagecoach

Many people made the long journey to the West by stagecoach. The journey could be an unforgettable adventure.

In the early 1800's, most people traveled by stagecoach. Travelers from Eastern cities journeyed to Ohio along the National Road in Concord coaches pulled by six horses. Many of the best coaches were made in Concord, New Hampshire.

In the West, stagecoach passengers faced a slow, uncomfortable, and sometimes dangerous journey. People in a hurry rode on horseback. But a coach was safer than riding alone. A group of coach passengers had a better chance of fighting off hostile Indians or bandits.

Humming wires

The first transcontinental telegraph line in the United States was completed in 1861. Before the telegraph, a letter sent from the East might take weeks to reach the West. Now a person could send a telegraph message in minutes.

A stagecoach thunders across the desert with Indians in pursuit. This painting, *Downing the Nigh Leader* by Frederic Remington, catches the drama and excitement of the Wild West.

A long and dusty road

The famous Butterfield Overland Mail ran four coaches a week between St. Louis and San Francisco. The coaches bumped along, day and night. The passengers, grimy with dust in summer and shivering with cold in winter, tried to sleep on the hard seats. Crude wood or adobe "stations" every 10 miles (16 kilometers) or so provided food for passengers and horses.

A famous name

Wells, Fargo & Company was founded in 1852 by Henry Wells and William G. Fargo to provide an East-West express stage service. When it bought out Benjamin Holladay's overland freight line in 1866, Wells, Fargo & Company became the most powerful firm in the West. It carried passengers, freight, and mail, and one of its special jobs was to ship gold from mines.

Railroads and Steamboats

The first transcontinental rail link across the United States was completed in 1869. This historic photograph shows the meeting of the Central Pacific and Union Pacific railroads at Promontory, Utah.

Railroads and steamboats carried supplies to settlers and miners in the West. By 1869, a railroad spanned the continent. The days of the wagon train were numbered.

The growth of railroads

The government thought railroads would attract settlers to the frontier territories. It gave land to companies seeking to build new railroad lines. In 1856, a railroad was built from the Great Lakes at Chicago south to the Gulf of Mexico at Mobile, Alabama. Settlers poured into lands along the route after the railroad was completed.

East meets West

In the 1860's, two companies began building the first railroad across America. The Union Pacific started from the east. Many of its workers were Irish. The Central Pacific line, coming from the west, included thousands of Chinese in its construction gangs. On May 10, 1869, the two tracks met at Promontory, near Ogden, Utah.

Other lines soon followed, including the Southern Pacific and the Atchison, Topeka, and Santa Fe. New towns were founded at the end of the tracks.

CAMELS IN THE WEST?

Strange but true. Some frontier people used camels, imported from Asia, because these animals could live in the desert. During the 1850's, the U.S. Army used camels to carry freight from Texas to California. Some of the camels escaped and roamed wild in Arizona until at least 1905.

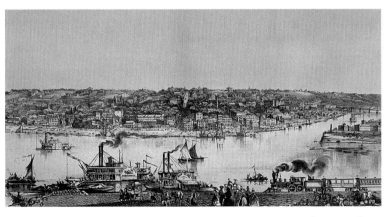

A Mississippi River port – Davenport, Iowa – in 1866. Steamboats and railroads brought people, supplies, and industry to the West.

Changing the West

The railroads changed the West. With railroads to supply them, settlers had less fear of waterless deserts or of hostile Indians. Trains linked frontier towns with Eastern cities, bringing in more settlers. Railroads also cut through the traditional buffalo-hunting grounds of the Plains Indians.

Steamboats

Paddlewheel steamboats chugged along waterways throughout the United States, and especially on the Mississippi and Missouri rivers. Gamblers and tricksters plied their trades on some boats, persuading miners and settlers to part with hard-earned money. Port cities thrived on river trade.

A stern-wheel steamboat

GREASE FROM THE GROUND

Wagon axles had to be greased to keep the wheels turning freely. In some places, pioneers found the oil they wanted seeping from the ground. In 1833, an oil spring was discovered in the Wind River Basin, Wyoming. Jim Bridger sold oil from his fort in Wyoming, and pioneers mixed it with flour to use as axle grease.

BULLWHACKERS AND MULESKINNERS

Before the railroads, wagons hauled heavy freight. A wagon train usually included about 25 wagons, each pulled by a team of 6 to 20 oxen or mules. The drivers were called bullwhackers or muleskinners. The wagons rumbled along slowly, covering about 100 miles (160 kilometers) a week. They hauled ore from mines, brought in machinery and blasting powder for the miners, and carried food and water to desert camps.

A Western railroad locomotive had a "cowcatcher" in front to clear the track of obstacles. This train ran on the Virginia & Truckee Line in Nevada.

Towns and Town Taming

Frontier towns grew fast. Helena, Montana, sprang up after gold was discovered at Last Chance Gulch in 1864. This was the town's main street two years later.

Frontier towns sprang up almost overnight. An early arrival in Bovard, Nevada, told how he passed through the town in the morning and noticed four or five tents. When he returned in the afternoon, Main Street was a mile long, and business was booming in a string of tent saloons!

Home, sweet home

Frontier towns provided few comforts. Wealthy people shipped in furniture, tableware, and wallpaper at great expense. Miners often papered their shacks with newspapers to make them warmer. Some of these old newspapers can still be read on the walls of crumbling buildings in deserted ghost towns.

Most mining camps became ghost towns of collapsing buildings and sagebrush when the miners moved on. If a town became fairly permanent, the people built wooden sidewalks on each side of the dirt streets, lined with hitching posts where riders could tie up their horses. Square false fronts made small buildings look bigger and more impressive.

Silver lining

Two miners in Treasure City, Nevada, made a shelter of rocks to keep out the winter weather. In the spring, they discovered that the walls of their rocky home contained high-grade silver ore, worth thousands of dollars!

The Wild West

Most families on the frontier lived quietly. But life was rough in mining camps and cattle towns. Gambling, drinking, and guns led to violent quarrels and robberies. Claim jumpers stole mine claims from their lawful owners. Tricksters "salted" mines – selling worthless holes after putting in small amounts of gold or silver.

On the range, rustlers stole cattle, driving them off to secret hideouts. Law officers could do little against large bands of rustlers. One story tells of a sheriff who returned from a robber's hideout looking triumphant. "Get your man?" someone asked. "No," the sheriff replied, "but I rode plumb through the place without getting shot."

Tombstone was the scene of the gunfight at the O.K. Corral in 1881 – a year before this photograph was taken.

Range wars and outlaws

On the open range, feuds and range wars often broke out between ranchers, sheep owners, and farmers. Gunmen such as Billy the Kid took part in these shootouts. Outlaw gangs robbed banks, trains, and stagecoaches. A few outlaws like Henry Plummer, the Younger brothers, the Daltons, and Frank and Jesse James became notorious. Sooner or later, most were shot or hanged.

The lawmen

Western law officers such as Wyatt Earp, Pat Garrett, and Bat Masterson became as famous as the outlaws they hunted down.

Wyatt Earp
Unlike some other gunfighters, Wyatt Earp lived to be an old man. He died in 1929.

Wyatt Earp was born in Illinois in 1848. He worked as a buffalo hunter before becoming a police officer in Wichita and Dodge City, Kansas. In 1879, he moved to Tombstone, Arizona, where he worked as a stagecoach guard, card dealer, and deputy United States marshal. In Tombstone, he and his brothers took part in the famous gunfight at the O.K. Corral.

A feud developed between Ike Clanton's gang and three of the Earp brothers – Wyatt, Virgil, and Morgan. Virgil was marshal of Tombstone. In October 1881, the Earps and their friend Doc Holliday shot to death three of Clanton's gang at the O.K. Corral. The Earps said they were trying to make an arrest. Others said it was murder.

Boom town

Virginia City, Nevada, grew rich on the gold and silver mines of the Comstock Lode. By 1876, this city of 21,000 people had 20 laundries, 6 churches, 150 saloons, an opera house, and several theaters.

At any time, a person in the city might find silver ore in the basement. Children running out to play ran the risk of tumbling into a new mine dug next door!

Billy the Kid

Outlaws and Rangers

The West was not as violent or lawless as stories and movies make out. But there were some real desperadoes, ready to steal and kill. Frontier peacekeepers like the Texas Rangers did their best to track down these criminals.

Billy the Kid

Billy the Kid was a killer and a cattle thief. He killed at least 5 people, though according to legends, the number of victims he shot dead was as many as 21.

The Kid's real name was Henry McCarty and he was born in New York City in 1859. He moved west with his family, and became a fugitive after shooting a man. He fled to Lincoln County, New Mexico, under the name William H. Bonney, and became a hired gun during the Lincoln County cattle war.

In 1880, Pat Garrett, sheriff of Lincoln County, caught up with Billy, his one-time friend. The Kid was tried and sentenced to death, but escaped from jail after killing two deputies. Sheriff Garrett tracked him to Fort Sumner, New Mexico, ambushed him in a darkened house, and shot him dead on July 14, 1881.

Pat Garrett was shot dead in 1908 by a rancher during a land dispute.

Jesse James

Jesse James was a bank and train robber, born in Clay County, Missouri, in 1847. During the Civil War (1861-1865) he and his older brother, Frank, joined bands of killers and thieves led by Southern Confederate sympathizers. After the war, the James boys joined their cousins, the Youngers, and began to hold up stagecoaches, trains, and banks.

In 1881, the Governor of Missouri offered a $5,000 reward for the arrest of Frank or Jesse. Robert Ford, a gang member, shot Jesse dead on April 3, 1882.

Jesse James

What were vigilantes?

Citizens in frontier towns sometimes banded together in groups called vigilantes to capture and punish criminals. Sometimes vigilantes killed innocent people in their rush to justice.

Belle Starr

Belle Starr

Belle Starr was born in Missouri in 1848, but moved to Texas when she was 16. There she married an outlaw named Jim Reed and had two children. Reed was killed in a gunfight, and several years later, Belle moved to the Indian Territory (now eastern Oklahoma) and married Sam Starr, a Cherokee Indian. Their cabin became a notorious outlaw hideout.

In 1883, Sam and Belle were found guilty of horse stealing, and she went to jail. Three years later, Sam Starr was shot in a fight. Belle then lived with Bill July, a part-Cherokee horse thief. In 1889, while July was in court, a gunman killed Belle in an ambush.

Judge Roy Bean

Judge Roy Bean (about 1825-1904) boasted he was the only "Law West of the Pecos."

Bean set up a saloon in the town of Langtry, at the end of the railroad in Texas. He called his saloon "The Jersey Lily" after he fell in love with a picture of the beautiful English actress Lily Langtry. He held court at one end of the bar, and relied on a single law book and his six-guns to keep order. He once fined a corpse $40 for carrying concealed weapons!

Roy Bean

Texas Rangers

The Texas Rangers

The Texas Rangers were organized officially in 1835 to protect American settlers in Texas from Indians and bandits. Rangers rode in companies but had no uniforms or regular pay. A Ranger learned to ride and track like a Comanche Indian, and was a good shot with a six-shooter. Texas Rangers hunted down murderers, smugglers, train and bank robbers, and mine bandits.

Today, Texas Rangers use modern methods to investigate crimes. But they still ride horses in pursuit of lawbreakers in rugged areas.

Indian Wars

Several Indian tribes were defeated at the Battle of Tippecanoe (1811) in Indiana.

After settlers came to their lands, many Native Americans fought for survival. Even peaceful tribes were forced to go to war. They fought an enemy who grew more powerful as more and more settlers moved to the West. Some whites were ready to kill all the Indians.

The Middle West

The Indians of the Midwest, south of the Great Lakes, had fought American colonists off and on since 1775. In the early 1800's, the Shawnee chief Tecumseh and his brother, known as the Shawnee Prophet, united several tribes against the settlers.

In 1811, the Indians were defeated by the army of William Henry Harrison, governor of the Indiana Territory. Harrison became a hero among settlers and was later elected President of the United States (1840). After Tecumseh died in 1813, Indian resistance in the Middle West crumbled. The Black Hawk War of 1832 was the last Indian war in the Middle West. Abraham Lincoln took part in this war but saw no action.

Tecumseh was chief of the Shawnee.

Wise man of the Cherokee

Sequoyah (1760?-1843) was a Cherokee who invented a system of writing for his own people. His chief aim was to record ancient Cherokee culture. Many Cherokee learned to read and write their own language as a result of his work.

In 1828, Sequoyah went to Washington, D.C. to represent the Western tribes, and helped settle quarrels that arose among the Cherokee who were moved to the Indian Territory. Sequoyah died in Mexico while searching for some lost members of his tribe.

Shoshone Indians on a reservation in Wyoming. The Shoshone were given land in 1868, in return for keeping the peace and helping settlers fight hostile tribes. This photograph was taken in 1870.

Last fight of the Seminole

In the South, the Creeks rose up in 1813, but they were defeated the following year by Andrew Jackson. The Seminole of Florida fought on through the 1830's. Their leader Osceola vowed to fight "till the last drop of Seminole blood has moistened the dust of his hunting ground." Osceola was captured in 1837, but the Seminole kept fighting until they were almost wiped out. Some survivors moved west; others took refuge in the swamps of the Everglades.

The Cherokee were forced to move west of the Mississippi River. This 1942 painting, *The Trail of Tears* by Robert Lindneux, shows families with their possessions on the trail.

The Trail of Tears

White settlers demanded the U.S. government move all Indians in the Southeast to land west of the Mississippi River. Among them were the Cherokee, one of the most prosperous and progressive tribes in the country. Some Cherokee owned plantations, while others were farmers. During the winter of 1838-1839, U.S. troops forced thousands of Cherokee to leave their homes and make the long, difficult journey to the Indian Territory, in what is now Oklahoma. Many Indians died on the journey, which came to be called the Trail of Tears.

War on the Plains

By 1849, the Sioux and other Plains Indians grew alarmed as more settlers crossed their lands. The Indians fought to keep out the invaders. So began the last great Indian Wars.

Settlers were moving through Wyoming into Montana, along the Bozeman Trail. In 1866, the Army built three forts to keep the trail open. Led by Red Cloud, the Sioux surrounded the forts and besieged them for almost two years in what became known as the "Circle of Death." In 1868, the Army agreed to pull out of the forts and some of the Sioux agreed to settle on a reservation in South Dakota.

However, in 1874, gold was found in the Black Hills of South Dakota. Thousands of settlers then entered the region, breaking the agreement with the Indians.

The **cavalry charge** – a 1907 painting, *On the Southern Plains*, by Frederic Remington.

The Sioux Wars

To the Sioux, the Black Hills were sacred. When the government told the Sioux to move onto the reservation, the Sioux leaders Sitting Bull and Crazy Horse refused. "We are an island of Indians in a lake of whites," declared Sitting Bull. He vowed the Indians would fight any soldiers sent to force them onto the reservation.

On June 17, 1876, the Sioux defeated General George Crook's troops at the Battle of the Rosebud in Montana. On June 25, the soldiers of the famous Indian fighter George A. Custer met up with a large group of Sioux and Cheyenne on the Little Bighorn River. The battle that followed became known as "Custer's Last Stand." All 210 soldiers under Custer's immediate command were killed. The Indians split up to escape Army forces pursuing them. Sitting Bull went north to Canada. Crazy Horse surrendered and was killed.

Sitting Bull (1834?-1890) led the Hunkpapa Sioux. He was a famous medicine man. He told Indian warriors they must fight to kill, rather than show off to prove how brave they were – otherwise they would lose all their lands to the white people.

THE STRANGE ONE

Crazy Horse (1844?-1877) led the Sioux and Cheyenne to victory at the Battle of the Rosebud in 1876, and eight days later defeated Custer at the Battle of the Little Bighorn. Crazy Horse was admired by his people for his unusual spiritual powers – the Sioux called him their "Strange One." He gave himself up to the U.S. Army in 1877, but was killed by a soldier while being forced into a jail cell.

The Southern Plains

Farther south, Indians were roused to anger by incidents such as the Sand Creek massacre of 1864, when militia in Colorado attacked a village and killed Indian warriors, women, and children. Arapaho, Comanche, Cheyenne, and Kiowa fought 14 battles against the Army during the Red River War of 1874-1875.

The Comanche fought on horseback. In battle, a Comanche sometimes evaded arrows and bullets by hanging against the side of – or even under – his horse. These Comanche warriors were drawn about 1836 by artist George Catlin.

CUSTER'S LAST STAND

Custer's regiment was part of a force commanded by General Alfred H. Terry. Army scouts discovered an Indian camp in a valley along the Little Bighorn River. Custer expected to find about 1,000 warriors there. In fact, there were 2,000.

- Custer split his cavalry into three groups. One group, led by Major Reno, attacked the Indian camp but was driven back. The second group, led by Captain Benteen, joined Reno's men on the hillside.

- Custer and his men were surrounded and wiped out. The Indians scattered next day.

- Custer's critics said he attacked rashly, without waiting for Terry's main force.

- Custer's supporters said Reno could have rescued Custer's men if he had not retreated.

Red Cloud was chief of the Oglala Sioux. He has been called the only Indian who ever won a war against the U.S. government. Red Cloud died in 1909 at the age of 87.

The Last Battles

Chief Joseph and the Nez Perce Indians eventually surrendered near the Canadian border.

The tide of white settlement threatened to sweep away the Indians. Outnumbered and outgunned, they were weakened by starvation and disease. The last battles of the Indian Wars were desperate attempts by Indians to fight off the future.

The Trek of the Nez Perce

In 1877, Chief Joseph of the Nez Perce refused to move his people from their home in Oregon to a reservation in Idaho. Joseph held off an Army force, but realized he could not defeat the much stronger enemy. He led a remarkable retreat of his people over 1,000 miles (1,600 kilometers) southeast through Montana and then north across Yellowstone Park.

The Indians escaped the Army several times as they tried to reach Canada, but they were caught close to the border and gave up after a five-day battle. The government sent the Nez Perce to live in the Indian Territory in Oklahoma. Chief Joseph ended his days on a reservation in Washington. He died in 1904.

Wars against the Navajo

Indians in the Southwest had fought the Spanish long before Americans began settling in Arizona and New Mexico. The U.S. government sent many expeditions against the Navajo, but fighting always broke out again. In 1864, Kit Carson and 400 men attacked the Navajo in their canyon stronghold, after killing many of their animals and destroying their crops. The Navajo were imprisoned in New Mexico until 1868.

Apache raiders

Raids by the Apache increased in the 1860's, when frontier Army posts were closed during the Civil War. The Apache hated reservation life. They were determined to live as they had always done – or die fighting. Cochise, Victorio, Mangas Coloradas, and Geronimo were among those who led small bands of Apaches in lightning attacks on lonely outposts. Soldiers were ordered to kill every Indian able to fight and capture all women and children. Even after Geronimo and his band gave up in 1886, raids by other Apache groups continued into the 1890's.

Geronimo led a band of Chiricahua Apache. He was captured several times, but escaped to fight again and again. Geronimo finally surrendered in 1886. He spent the rest of his life at Fort Sill in Oklahoma, and died in 1909.

A cavalry attack on an Indian camp is shown in this painting (about 1900).

The Ghost Dance

The Ghost Dance was a religious movement that gave hope to despairing Indians. Its founders included Wovoka, a Paiute Indian who in a trance saw a peaceful future in which the buffalo herds returned to the Plains. Central to the movement was a ceremony called the Ghost Dance, in which dancers fell into trances and saw visions. Dancers wore special shirts that some warriors believed would protect them from enemy bullets.

By 1890, the Ghost Dance was spreading among Plains Indians living on reservations. Fearful that the movement would lead to more fighting, the Army tried to arrest the Sioux leader, Sitting Bull, who was killed. The Ghost Dance movement faded away after soldiers massacred Indians at Wounded Knee Creek. The old life of the Plains had gone forever. Wovoka lived on until 1932.

At Wounded Knee, more than 200 Indians were massacred by soldiers. In December 1890, about 350 Lakota Sioux surrendered near Wounded Knee Creek in South Dakota. Troops surrounded them. Someone fired a shot, and the soldiers began firing on the Indians. This was the last battle of the Indian Wars.

The death of Sitting Bull. In 1890, Sitting Bull helped start the Ghost Dance movement. Indian police officers were sent to arrest the Sioux chief. He and his son were killed. This 1890 print shows Sitting Bull falling from his horse during the skirmish.

Travel far, fight fiercely

The Apaches earned their reputation. In 1885, 11 Apache warriors escaped from a reservation. In four weeks, they covered more than 1,200 miles (1,930 kilometers), killed 38 people, and captured 250 horses and mules. The Army chased them into Mexico.

A Western Legend

"Remember the Alamo" became a battle cry in Texas. The famous siege of the mission building has become part of Western legend.

The Alamo stands in San Antonio, Texas. From 1718, the building was used as a Roman Catholic mission. Its popular name, the Alamo, came from the Spanish name for the cottonwood trees that grew around it. The mission was sometimes used as a fort.

The Alamo remembered. People attend a memorial service at the Alamo. The mission is now a restored historic site.

The Texans revolt

During the winter of 1835-1836, the people of Texas decided to break with Mexico, which then governed Texas. General Antonio López de Santa Anna led a Mexican army to crush the revolt. The Texan commander, William Barret Travis, and about 150 Texans prepared to defend San Antonio.

The siege

Among the Texans were the famous frontiersmen James Bowie and Davy Crockett. Faced with 4,000 Mexican troops, Travis and his men retreated into the Alamo. Another small group of men slipped through the Mexican lines, swelling the number of Alamo defenders to 189 men. The siege of the Alamo lasted 13 days. By then, the defenders were so low on bullets they could no longer return fire. The Mexicans climbed the walls and the siege ended in hand-to-hand fighting. On the morning of March 6, the Mexicans captured the fort.

Davy Crockett dressed in hunting clothes to have this picture painted by John Chapman in 1834.

DAVY CROCKETT

Davy Crockett (1786-1836) was born in Tennessee. As an Army scout, he fought the Creek Indians. In the 1820's, he became a politician and was elected to the U.S. House of Representatives. After he lost an election in 1835, he set out for Texas, hoping to revive his fortunes, only to be killed at the Alamo.

Crockett was famous for tall tales. Stories written about him after his death boosted the legend of a frontier hero who could "run faster, jump higher, squat lower, dive deeper, stay under longer, and come out drier than any man in the whole country!"

BOWIE'S KNIFE

James Bowie (1796?-1836) died at the Alamo. He gave his name to the bowie knife. Bowie is said to have added the long bolster, an upright piece adjoining the knife handle, after he lost his grip on a butcher knife in an Indian fight.

The bowie knife was used for hunting and as a weapon.

The fight for the Alamo. This 1903 painting, *The Fall of the Alamo*, by Robert Onderdonk, shows Davy Crockett using his empty rifle as a club. He and 188 other defenders held off a Mexican army for nearly two weeks.

Few survivors

All the Alamo fighters were killed. Some historians believe that Davy Crockett and a few defenders were captured, only to be executed at Santa Anna's orders. Others accept that all the Texans who fought died in the battle. Among the survivors were Susanna Dickinson, an officer's wife; her baby; and Travis's black slave Joe.

Defeat becomes victory

The heroic fight at the Alamo had given General Sam Houston time to gather a Texan army. He retreated eastward, pursued by Santa Anna, and then turned on the Mexicans on the afternoon of April 21, while most of the enemy soldiers were resting. The Battle of San Jacinto lasted just 18 minutes. The Texans captured or killed most of the Mexican troops, and won their independence.

Sharpshooters

THE SIX-SHOOTER

Samuel Colt (1814-1862) developed the first successful repeating pistol in 1835. It could fire up to six shots before being reloaded.

Later Colt handguns included the Colt Walker and the single-action Army revolver.

Six-guns were usually carried in holsters on gunbelts. Small guns known as Derringers, made by Henry Derringer, Jr., could be carried in a bag or hidden in a coat pocket.

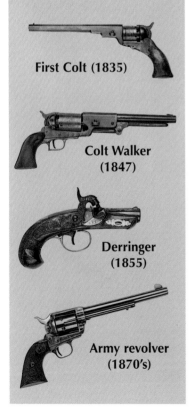

First Colt (1835)

Colt Walker (1847)

Derringer (1855)

Army revolver (1870's)

The sharpshooter became part of the Western legend. Truth was often more surprising than fiction.

Wild Bill Hickok

James Butler Hickok was born in Illinois in 1837. As a youth, he learned to be a crack shot and a tough fighter. He had many jobs – farmworker, stagecoach driver, wagon master, and gambler. During the Civil War (1861-1865), he served the Union as a spy and scout. In 1867, he scouted for Custer's Seventh Cavalry.

Hickok was then elected sheriff of Ellis County, Kansas, and lived in the wild frontier town of Hays City. Later, as marshal of Abilene, he shot and killed a gambler, and, by mistake, a policeman. The citizens of Abilene decided not to reelect him.

Wild Bill then drifted, gambling and performing in a play called *Scouts of the Prairie* with Buffalo Bill. In 1876, he moved to Deadwood in the Dakota Territory, hoping to strike gold. There he was shot and killed while playing cards. Wild Bill Hickok fell to the floor still clutching a pair of aces and eights, known ever since as the "dead man's hand."

Wild Bill Hickok

Annie Oakley

Annie Oakley (1860-1926) was a crack shot and a star of Buffalo Bill's Wild West show. During her act, she shot a coin out of her husband's hand or a cigarette out of his mouth. She could also hit a playing card tossed into the air 90 feet (27 meters) away.

Annie Oakley's real name was Phoebe Ann Moses. She was born in Ohio and learned to shoot at the age of 8. When only 15, she outshot Frank Butler, an ace marksman, in a contest. In 1876, she and Butler married, and they later toured America and Europe until she left the Wild West show in 1901. Offstage, she preferred the quiet life, spending her time sewing rather than shooting.

Annie Oakley

Buffalo Bill

William Frederick Cody found fame as Buffalo Bill. Born in Iowa in 1846, he became a Pony Express rider in 1860. During the Civil War, Cody drove wagons for Kansas militia supporting the Union. He tried running a hotel, and then a freight business – until Indians captured his wagons and horses. He went to work on the new railroad and became a buffalo hunter, supplying meat for construction workers. His skill with a hunting rifle earned him the nickname Buffalo Bill.

From 1868 to 1872, Buffalo Bill scouted for the Army during the Indian Wars. Next he turned to show business, appearing in Wild West theatrical shows and in the play *Scouts of the Prairie*. In between, he went back to the Plains, where in 1876 he killed and scalped an Indian chief named Yellow Hand. Journalists wrote dramatic stories of his adventures, making him famous in the East.

In 1883, he formed a show called Buffalo Bill's Wild West. It featured cowboys, wagons, and a mock battle with Indians. Sitting Bull toured briefly with the show. The Wild West was a great success, touring the United States and Europe. Buffalo Bill went on performing until shortly before his death in 1917.

Buffalo Bill, from a painting by the French artist Rosa Bonheur.

Calamity Jane

No one is sure how Martha Canary (1852-1903) came to be known as Calamity Jane. According to one story, she used to warn men that to offend her was to court calamity!

She was raised in mining camps after her parents split up, and learned to ride and shoot. She usually dressed in men's clothes as she moved between frontier forts. Many wild stories exist about her – most of which she made up herself – but it is possible she scouted for Custer's Seventh Cavalry.

In 1875, she went to the Black Hills of South Dakota, seeking gold. She lived in Deadwood where she won praise for helping to treat victims of a smallpox outbreak. She performed in Wild West shows, displaying her skill as a rider and sharpshooter.

Legacy of the West

The frontier is gone. Great cities such as Denver and Salt Lake City now stand where settlers once pitched their tents. But Western frontier life left behind a great American tradition.

The end of the frontier

Changes on the Great Plains after the 1870's ended the era of the open range. New types of windmills allowed farmers to pump up water from deep underground. Barbed wire, first sold in 1874, cost less than wood, and soon large areas of open range were fenced in by wire.

Only the Indian Territory – now Oklahoma – remained untouched. White settlers demanded that the government open this area to them. In 1889, the government opened a large area of the Indian Territory for settlement. A wild land rush followed. More and more Indian Territory land was taken over. In 1890, the government declared that no frontiers remained in the United States. The settling of the American West was over.

Rodeo shows still thrill spectators. Barrel-racing is a women's rodeo event. The first rodeo to charge admission and offer prizes was held in Prescott, Arizona, in 1888. Cowboys formed the first professional rodeo organization in 1936.

Dodge City, Kansas, where cowboys once celebrated after the cattle drive. Visitors now take photographs of this restoration of Front Street.

The frontier experience

The West shaped many American ideas. Pioneer communities were simpler than those of the East. Frontier people shared hardships and relied on their own skills to make the things they needed. They built their own houses, produced their own food, and shared in decision-making.

The West offered success to those who worked hard. Frontier people were usually hopeful about the future. They moved on if they were not satisfied. Many immigrants settling in the West soon lost their attachment to their old homelands, and saw themselves as Americans.

Nature's bounty

The West had vast natural wealth. Unfortunately, the pioneers were often wasteful of these rich natural resources. They cut down forests, lost large amounts of gold and silver through careless mining, and wore out the soil with poor farming methods.

Memories of the silver rush. Virginia City, Nevada, is a Western ghost town. Tourists now wander through the settlement that grew overnight when silver prospectors flocked to Nevada in the 1860's.

Cowboys still ride the range but the wild longhorn cattle have gone. Modern beef breeds are raised on this ranch in Wyoming.

Artists and writers were fascinated by the West. Their stories and pictures brought the excitement and spirit of the West to people living in faraway cities.

Western artist

Frederic Remington (1861-1909) painted and drew over 2,700 pictures of the West. He experienced life on the frontier, visiting Montana in 1881 and returning to the West many times from his home in the East. Remington was also a sculptor. His figure of the *Bronco Buster* is typical of his action-filled style.

Bronco Buster by Frederic Remington shows a cowboy riding an unbroken mustang.

Approaching Chimney Rock is a 1930 painting by William Henry Jackson. The artist shows wagons forming a circle as the settlers prepare to camp for the night.

The outlaw Jesse James, according to an old ballad, "killed many a man, and robbed the Glendale train." This scene was painted in 1936 by Thomas Hart Benton, an artist noted for his Western pictures. It forms part of a mural or wall-painting in the State Capitol at Jefferson City, Missouri.

A short-lived legend

The galloping riders of the Pony Express also inspired stories and paintings – even though this mail delivery service had just a brief history.

The Pony Express started from St. Joseph, Missouri – then the western end of the railroad system. Its young riders set out to deliver letters and small packages to California in 10 days or less – faster than any other mail service of that time.

The Pony Express lasted just 19 months. It made its first run on April 3, 1860. On October 24, 1861, the first telegraph service across the continent opened. The Pony Express, unable to compete, closed two days later.

A Pony Express rider changes horses in Frederic Remington's painting *The Coming and Going of the Pony Express*. A Pony Express rider changed horses in about two minutes. He rode about 75 miles (121 kilometers), before another rider took over.

PONY EXPRESS FACTS

- Riders rode day and night between relay stations 10 to 15 miles (15 to 24 kilometers) apart, mounting a fresh horse at each stop.

- The total route of the Pony Express was 1,966 miles (3,164 kilometers).

- Only one Pony Express rider was killed by Indians.

- The fastest run was in March 1861. A copy of President Abraham Lincoln's first address to Congress arrived in Sacramento, California, just 7 days and 17 hours after leaving St. Joseph.

- In winter, delivery often took up to 15 days.

Stories and movies about the West tell of the land and people – especially pioneers, cowboys, and Indians. Children enjoy tales of the heroes of Western folklore. In the modern world, the story of the West has moved on to a new chapter.

Western books

There have been many books about the West. Most of the early stories came from people who had been there – like Mark Twain, whose *Roughing It* became a frontier classic. Andy Adams, himself a cowboy, gave a realistic account of range life in *The Log of a Cowboy*.

Zane Grey wrote more than 50 exciting Western novels including *Riders of the Purple Sage* (1912). Later Western writers include Louis L'Amour (*Hondo*), Jack Schaefer (*Shane*), and Larry McMurtry (*Lonesome Dove*).

The West on screen

Hollywood has produced many films about the West, and some of the biggest stars in movie history made their names by riding horses and shooting guns in exciting adventures. Directors such as John Ford made the Western landscape a dramatic background for their films. The best Western movies became film classics. Children all over the world copied Western movies, and played their own Western games – good guys against the bad.

The magnificent scenery of the West thrills movie audiences and tourists. Beautiful rock formations rise from the floor of Monument Valley in Arizona.

Tom Mix was a cowboy star of the silent movies.

John Wayne was the tough-guy hero of many Westerns.

Gary Cooper starred in the Western classic *High Noon*.

PAUL BUNYAN AND PECOS BILL

These heroes of Western folklore are famous for their strength and amazing deeds. People still enjoy hearing the stories about them.

Paul Bunyan was a lumberjack. He scooped out the Great Lakes to provide drinking water for Babe, his giant blue ox.

Pecos Bill was born in eastern Texas. He fell out of the family wagon near the Pecos River, and was raised by coyotes. He taught broncos how to buck!

To win a bet, Pecos Bill once rode an Oklahoma cyclone without a saddle. The cyclone could not throw him and finally "rained out" from under him in Arizona. The rain fell so heavily that it created the Grand Canyon. Bill crashed in California, and his fall left a hole – Death Valley.

DID YOU KNOW?

New books, stories, paintings, songs, plays, and movies about the West appear every year. Almost 450 works have been produced about Billy the Kid alone! They include poems, novels, plays, ballets, and movies.

Indians in the United States

In books and movies, the Indians were often beaten by the cowboys. The cowboy heroes then rode away to new adventures. But what happened to the Indians? Their traditional way of life was gone forever.

After 1887, Indian tribal lands were broken up into small units for farms. However, few Indians were interested in farming. Many sold their land or were cheated out of it.

Today, about 2 million Native Americans live in the United States. About a third live on reservations or tribal lands, and preserve their old cultures, though under pressure from the modern world. Fewer Indian languages are spoken today, and the movement of Indians from reservations to cities has weakened traditional values.

Campaigners for Native American rights have demanded greater control of their own affairs, and gone to court to regain lost lands or receive payment for them.

Indian dance at Frontier Days, Wyoming. Native Americans maintain their traditions through dances and festivals.

61

Glossary

adobe Brick made of sun-dried clay.

bandit An outlaw, a person who steals from others.

Basque Someone from the Basque region of the Pyrenees Mountains between France and Spain.

buckskin Soft leather made from the hide of a deer.

ceremony A formal act performed on a special occasion.

coonskin Fur taken from a raccoon, a small animal with a long, black-ringed tail.

dung Droppings of animals. Buffalo dung was burned as fuel in the West.

fort A building made to defend people inside from attack. Western forts had walls of mud-brick or wooden poles.

frontier The boundary between settled land and unsettled land.

gambler A person who bets on the results of a game or contest, for example by playing cards for money.

gold rush A mass movement of people into a region seeking gold.

holster Case for carrying a pistol, often made of leather and worn on a belt.

homestead A piece of public land granted to a settler to use as a home and farm.

immigrant A person who comes from the country of his or her birth to live in a foreign land.

interpreter A person who translates from one language into another.

keelboat A flat-bottomed boat.

lariat A cowboy's rope.

liquor Alcoholic drink such as whiskey or rum.

lodge A Native American dwelling.

longhorn Original half-wild cattle of the West, named for their long horns.

marshal A law officer appointed by the federal government.

massacre Cruel and bloody killing of large numbers of people.

meal Grain that has been ground into tiny pieces.

mirage An optical illusion sometimes seen at sea or in hot deserts. It gives the appearance of something that is not really there.

mission Place where missionaries work, often used as a church and school.

missionary A person sent out by a religious group to teach religion or to help set up schools and hospitals.

mustang Small wild horse of the western plains of North America.

nugget A lump of metal ore.

packhorse A horse used to carry loads.

pass A road or way through difficult country, especially through mountains.

pelt The skin of a fur-bearing animal, such as a wolf or beaver, used for making clothes and rugs.

pemmican Meat that has been dried, pounded, and mixed with fat to preserve it.

pioneer A person who is the first to settle in a region.

prospector A person who searches an area to discover valuable minerals and ores.

range Open country used to raise herds of cattle.

reservation Land set aside by U.S. government for Native Americans to live on.

rustler A cattle thief.

sagebrush Shrub plant of the dry plains, sometimes blown by the wind.

saloon Place of entertainment with a bar, card games, and music.

scalp The skin on top of the head.

scout Someone sent out to get and bring back information.

settler Someone who goes to live in a new land.

shaman Medicine man or priest.

sheriff A law officer in a county.

stagecoach Horse-drawn coach that carried passengers, mail, and freight.

stampede A sudden rush of a herd of startled animals.

stirrup Leather or metal hoop that hangs down from the side of a saddle to hold the rider's foot.

surveyor A person who measures land to identify its features.

telegraph Communications system for sending messages in code through electrical wires.

tepee A cone-shaped tent made by stretching animal skins or tree bark over tall poles.

territory An area of land, often land that is unexplored or does not have the same rights and privileges as a state or province.

trailblazer Explorer who makes a new trail through wild country, marking the way by cuts on the bark of trees or signs scratched on rocks.

trapper A person who catches wild animals in traps.

wickiup Native American dwelling made from brushwood.

wigwam Native American dwelling made of poles covered with hides, bark, or woven mats.

Index A page number in **bold** type indicates a picture

Picture acknowledgments

Cover: Bettmann Archive; L. Burton, H. Armstrong Roberts; The Smithsonian Institution, Washington D.C.; Brown Brothers; The Westen Pacific Railroad Company

Back Cover: Frederick Remington Art Museum, Ogdensburg, N.Y.; Oklahoma Historical Society; National Archives, Washington D.C.

1 National Museum of Natural History; rifle, Phil Spangenberger Collection (Roger Roland Fuhr, ROLANDesign). 3 Field Museum of Natural History, Chicago, WORLD BOOK photo; Roger Roland Fuhr, ROLANDesign. 4 Woolaroc Museum, Bartlesville, Okla.; L. Burton, H. Armstrong Roberts. 5 Currier and Ives lithograph (detail), Bettmann Archive. 6 Detail of *A Skin Lodge of an Assiniboine Chief*, The Newberry Library, Chicago, Edward E. Ayer Collection. 7 The Smithsonian Institution, Washington, D.C.; buffalo photo © Robert E. Pelham, Bruce Coleman. 8 *Prairie Scene Mirage* by Alfred Jacob Miller, Walters Art Gallery, Baltimore, Md. 9 Detail of *Indian Hunters Pursuing the Buffalo* by Peter Rindisbacher, Peabody Museum of Archeology and Ethnology, Harvard University, Cambridge, Mass. 10 Painting by Alfred Jacob Miller, Walters Art Gallery, Baltimore, Md.; Engraving of Johnny Appleseed from *History of Ashland County* frontispiece, J. B. Lippincott & Co., Philadelphia, Chicago Historical Society. 11 *Daniel Boone Escorting Settlers Through the Cumberland Gap*, Washington University Gallery of Art, St. Louis. 12 Independence National Historic Park Collection, Philadelphia. 12-13 Jeff Gnass, West Stock. 13 Bridger, Kansas State Historical Society; Carson, Culver; Frémont engraving by J. C. Fry, Chicago Historical Society. 14 *The Interior of the Hut of a Mandan Chief*, Rare Book Division, New York Public Library, Astor, Lenox and Tilden Foundations. 15 *A Comanche Village*, The Smithsonian Institution, Washington, D.C.; *Winter Games of the Cheyenne*, Philbrook Art Center, Tulsa, Okla. 16 Lauren Freudmann, Woodfin Camp, Inc.; *Sioux Sun Dance* by Oscar Howe, Philbrook Art Center, Tulsa, Okla. Gift of Clark Field. 17 *Navajo Weavers* by Harrison Begay, Philbrook Art Center, Tulsa, Okla.; Dr. Georg Gerster, Photo Researchers. 18 Richard Erdoes, Alpha; detail of *Indians Hunting Buffalo with Bows and Lances* by George Catlin, The Newberry Library, Chicago, Edward E. Ayer Collection. 19 Buffalo dance by Karl Bodmer, Joslyn Art Museum, Omaha, Nebr.; Bodmer drawing from *Travels in the Interior of North America 1832-1834* by Prince Maximilian of Wied, the Schweitzer Gallery, New York City. 20 The Smithsonian Institution, Washington, D.C.; sketch by Karl Bodmer, Joslyn Art Museum, Omaha, Nebr., Northern Natural Gas Company Collection; tomahawks, National Museum of Natural History, The Smithsonian Institution, Washington, D.C. 21 Detail of *A Bird's Eye View of the Mandan Village*, The Smithsonian Institution, Washington, D.C., WORLD BOOK photo by Robert Crandall; Sioux chief, oil painting on canvas (1832) by George Catlin, National Museum of American Art, Smithsonian Institution, Washington, D.C.; shield cover from Field Museum of Natural History, Chicago, WORLD BOOK photo. 23 Thomas Birch painting, Wadsworth Atheneum, Hartford, Conn., bequest of Mrs. Clara Hinton Gould; *The Camden and Amboy Railroad with the Engine "Planet" in 1834* by Edward Lamson Henry, Graham Gallery, New York City. 24 Bob McNerling, Taurus. 24-25 *Emigrant Train Fording Medicine Bow Creek, Rocky Mountains*, Bennington Museum, Bennington, Vt. (Gail McCullough). 26 Granger Collection. 28 Wood engraving (1867) by an unknown artist, Granger Collection. 31 Bettmann Archive; rifle, Phil Spangenberger Collection (Roger Roland Fuhr, ROLANDesign). 32 California State Library. 33 Loveland Museum, Loveland, Colo., reproduced with permission of *The Denver Post*.; (bottom) National Cowboy Hall of Fame, California. 34 Kansas State Historical Society; Library of Congress. 35 The Thomas Gilcrease Institute of American History and Art, Tulsa, Okla. 36 UP/Bettmann Archive. 37 *Texas Longhorns*, painting by Tom Lea, Dallas Museum of Art, Texas; UP/Bettmann Archive. 38-39 Courtesy J. B. Lippincott Company from *Frederic Remington* by Harold McCracken. 40 Union Pacific Railroad; Putnam Museum. 41 The Western Pacific Railroad Company. 42 Montana Historical Society. 43 Arizona Historical Society Library; Montgomery Foto Service. 44 Brown Bros.; Missouri Historical Society. 45 Oklahoma Historical Society; Brown Bros.; Archives Division, Texas State Library. 46 Lithograph (1889), Indiana Historical Society; Granger Collection. 47 Bureau of American Ethnology, Smithsonian Institution; detail of *The Trail of Tears*, Woolaroc Museum, Bartlesville, Okla. 48 Metropolitan Museum of Art, New York City (gift of several gentlemen); Brown Bros. 49 The Newberry Library, Chicago, Edward E. Ayer Collection; Brown Bros.; Smithsonian Institution. 50 National Archives, Washington, D.C. 51 *Attack at Dawn* by Charles Schreyvogel, Thomas Gilcrease Institute of American History and Art, Tulsa, Okla.; *Capture and Death of Sitting Bull*, lithograph by Kurz and Allison, Denver Public Library. 52 © Bob Daemmrich; Crockett painting, Humanities Research Center, University of Texas, Austin. 53 David R. Frazier Photolibrary; detail of *Fall of the Alamo*, Governor's Mansion of Texas (Friends of the Governor's Mansion). 54 (guns) Roger Roland Fuhr, ROLANDesign, Los Angeles; Kansas State Historical Society; Bettmann Archive. 55 Buffalo Bill painting, Whitney Museum of Western Art, Cody, Wyo.; Culver. 56 Rodeo © Thomas Woodrich, Hillstrom Stock Photo; Dodge City © James Blank, West Stock; ranching, Wyoming Travel Commission. 57 Bob and Ira Spring. 58 Bronze sculpture (1895) Frederic Remington Art Museum, Ogdensurg, New York; Scotts Bluff National Monument, Nebraska. 59 Greg Leech, Missouri Department of Natural Resources; painting (1900) Thomas Gilcrease Institute of American History and Art, Tulsa, Okla. 60 David A. Barnes, Stock Market; (bottom, left to right) Culver; Warner Bros. Inc.; UPI. 61 Tom Stack & Associates.

Illustrations
By WORLD BOOK artists including Robert Addison, Lorence F. Bjorklund, Kevin Chadwick, H. Charles McBarron, Walter Maslon, and Anthony Saris.